THE WORLD OF
Geography

THE WORLD OF
Geography

WORLD INTERNATIONAL PUBLISHING LIMITED
MANCHESTER

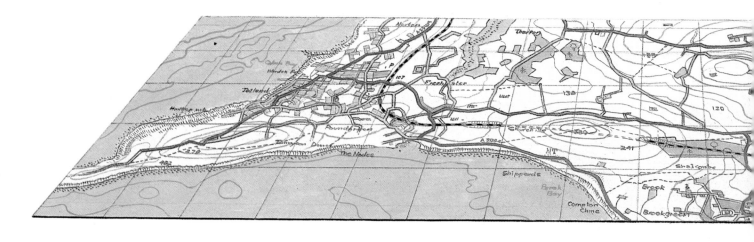

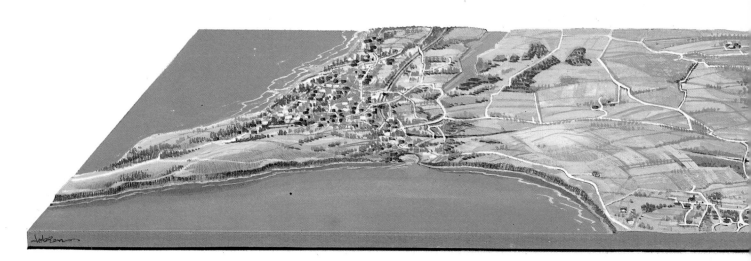

Contents

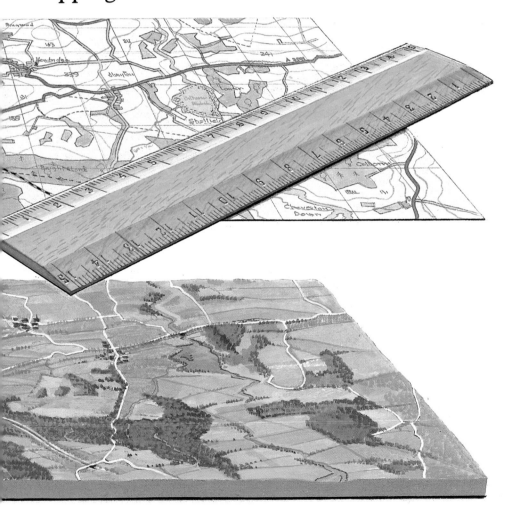

Birth of the Earth

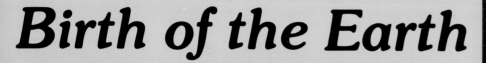

Most scientists now agree that the Earth was formed from a cloud of gas and dust. This cloud was drifting through space about 5000 million years ago. Gradually, more and more particles were drawn to the centre by gravity. There, about 4600 million years ago, they formed a star, the Sun. The material left over formed the planets, moons and other bodies that make up the Solar System

Above: The Earth is made up of three parts. The thin crust varies between 60-70 km thick under the highest montains to about 5 km thick under the oceans. Beneath the crust is the denser (heavier) mantle. The mantle is about 2900 km thick. It encloses the extremely dense core, which measures about 6920 km across. The inner core is solid, but the outer core is probably liquid.

The Earth's Early History

The youthful Earth was probably a huge ball of gas, rather like Jupiter or Saturn. But eventually, because of gravity, heavier elements, notably iron, sank towards the centre, forming a dense core, while lighter elements stayed near the surface. As a result, the Earth now has a very dense (heavy) core, made up largely of iron and nickel, a dense mantle and a relatively light crust.

The Earth slowly shrank into the rocky planet we know today. At first, the surface was hot and molten. Geologists have not found any rocks much older than about 3800 million years, although the Earth itself is about 4550 million years old. Rocks formed in the first 700 million years were probably all broken up and remelted.

The Earth's first atmosphere was poisonous, but it contained water vapour released from the rocks by volcanoes. It contained little oxygen, the gas we need to breathe. The oxygen content began to increase about 1900 million years ago, when oxygen-producing plants first developed.

Below: For many millions of years after its formation, the Earth's surface must have been blazing hot. Constant volcanic activity released gas and water vapour from the rocks inside the Earth. The gases formed a primitive and poisonous atmosphere. Later on, when the surface started to cool, there were great thunderstorms. Rain started to fill up hollows in the early crust. It was perhaps in these warm pools that the first living things, bacteria, appeared.

THE EARTH'S DIMENSIONS

DIAMETER: The equatorial diameter is 12,756 km, but the polar diameter is shorter, 12,713 km.

CIRCUMFERENCE: The equatorial circumference (the distance around the equator) is 40,075 km. But if you travel around the Earth via the poles (the polar circumference), the distance is only 40,007 km.

AREA: The Earth has an area of 510,066,000 km^2.

LAND AND SEA: The oceans cover 361,740,000 km^2. This is nearly 71 per cent of the Earth's surface.

Ages of the Earth

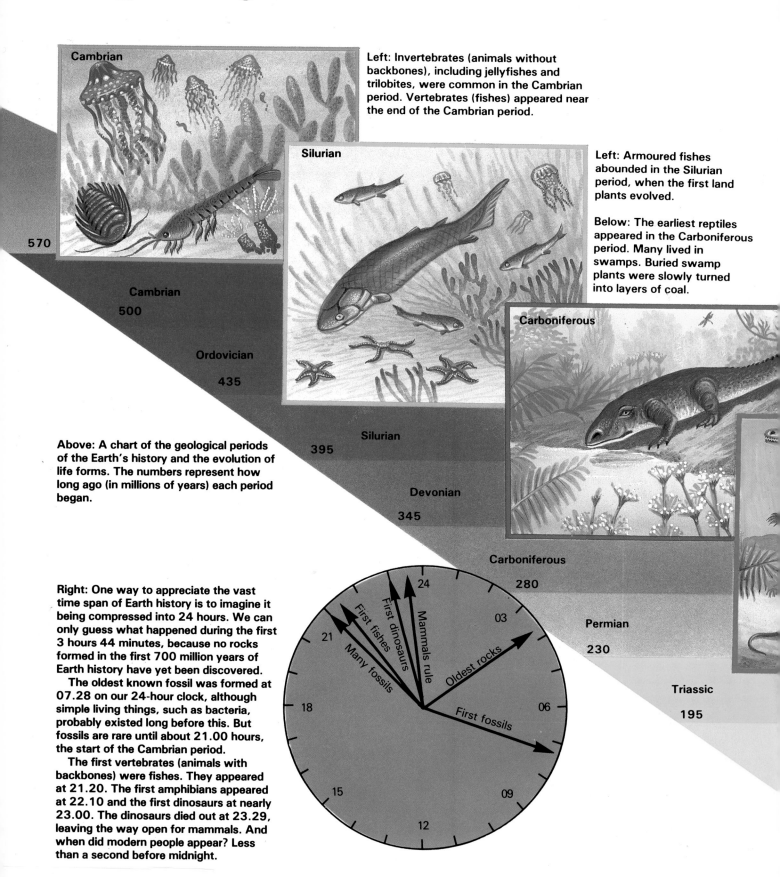

Left: Invertebrates (animals without backbones), including jellyfishes and trilobites, were common in the Cambrian period. Vertebrates (fishes) appeared near the end of the Cambrian period.

Left: Armoured fishes abounded in the Silurian period, when the first land plants evolved.

Below: The earliest reptiles appeared in the Carboniferous period. Many lived in swamps. Buried swamp plants were slowly turned into layers of coal.

570

Cambrian

500

Ordovician

435

Silurian

395

Devonian

345

Carboniferous

280

Permian

230

Triassic

195

Above: A chart of the geological periods of the Earth's history and the evolution of life forms. The numbers represent how long ago (in millions of years) each period began.

Right: One way to appreciate the vast time span of Earth history is to imagine it being compressed into 24 hours. We can only guess what happened during the first 3 hours 44 minutes, because no rocks formed in the first 700 million years of Earth history have yet been discovered.

The oldest known fossil was formed at 07.28 on our 24-hour clock, although simple living things, such as bacteria, probably existed long before this. But fossils are rare until about 21.00 hours, the start of the Cambrian period.

The first vertebrates (animals with backbones) were fishes. They appeared at 21.20. The first amphibians appeared at 22.10 and the first dinosaurs at nearly 23.00. The dinosaurs died out at 23.29, leaving the way open for mammals. And when did modern people appear? Less than a second before midnight.

8

Dating Rocks

The study of fossils made possible the fixing of the relative ages of rocks. And in the early 20th century, the discovery of radioactivity enabled scientists to fix the absolute ages of rocks. This is because some rocks contain bits of radioactive material which decays, or breaks down, at a fixed rate. Therefore, when scientists measure the proportion of a radioactive substance that has decayed, they can establish its age.

Eras and Periods

The last 570 million years are divided into the Palaeozoic (ancient life), Mesozoic (middle life) and Cenozoic (recent life) eras.

The Palaeozoic era (570-230 million years ago) is divided into six periods, although US geologists divide the Carboniferous period into two: the Mississippian and Pennsylvanian periods. The first period of the Palaeozoic era is the Cambrian. Cambrian rocks are rich in fossils. But in Precambrian rocks, formed before the Cambrian period began, fossils are rare. The Palaeozoic era saw the appearance of the first vertebrates (fishes), amphibians and reptiles.

The Mesozoic era (230-65 million years ago), contains three periods. It saw the rise of reptiles, including huge dinosaurs. Most reptiles became extinct at the end of the era.

The Cenozoic era in the last 65 million years saw the rise of mammals. This era contains two periods: the Tertiary and the Quaternary. Mighty mountain ranges such as the Alps and Himalayas were born during this era.

Above: The British Isles would look like this if the sea level rose or if the land sank by only 60 metres. The land and sea have changed many times throughout Earth history.

Triassic

Left: The first dinosaurs appeared in the Triassic period. The first mammals also evolved at this time.

Jurassic

Below left: The Jurassic period saw the emergence of such dinosaurs as *Brontosaurus* and *Stegosaurus*. There were flying reptiles, called Pterosaurs, and the first bird, *Archaeopteryx*.

Below: The Tertiary and Quaternary periods were dominated by mammals, such as giant ground sloths, huge grazing animals, sabre-toothed tigers and many birds. Primates date back 60 million years. Modern people (who are primates) appeared about 50,000 years ago.

Tertiary

Jurassic

Cretaceous

65

Tertiary

1.8

Quaternary

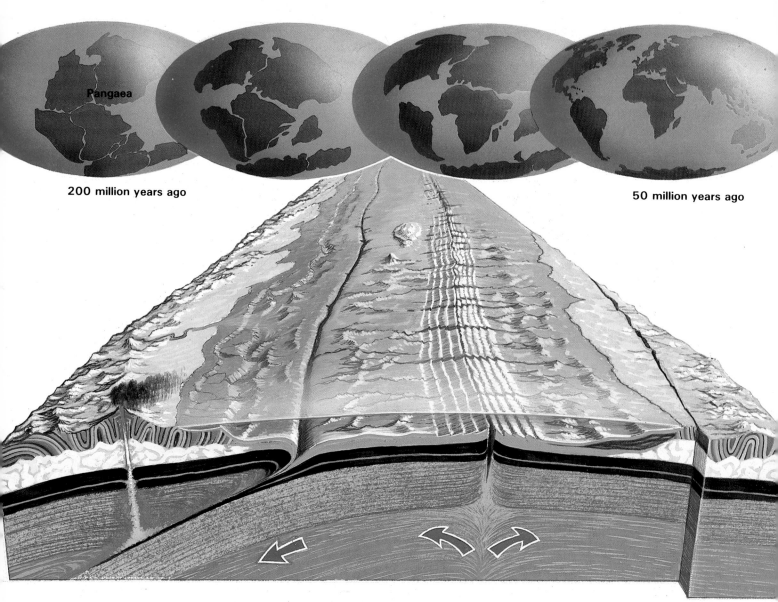

Pangaea

200 million years ago

50 million years ago

The Earth Beneath

Look at a map of the Atlantic Ocean. You will see that North and South America look as though they would fit together with Europe and Africa, like pieces in a jigsaw. About 70 years ago, some scientists suggested that the continents were once joined together.

A German, Alfred Wegener (1880-1930), found similar rock structures on the edges of the facing continents. Fossils of the same land animals, which lived around 200 million years ago, were dug up in South America and Africa. How did they get there? They could not have swum the ocean. Wegener was convinced that the continents had been joined together 200 million years ago. But how do continents move?

Top: the maps show how the world has changed over the last 200 million years.

Above: The diagram shows an ocean ridge rising from the sea floor. In the centre of these ridges are valleys. These valleys are the edges of plates. Semi-molten material in the upper mantle is rising beneath the ridges. Under the plates it divides and flows sideways, pulling the plates apart. As the plates move, molten material wells up to fill the gap. It hardens into new crustal rock.

Along the deep ocean trenches, the fluid material sinks dowards and one plate is pushed beneath another. The diagram shows plates moving apart and plates colliding. Other plates move alongside each other. Such plates are separated by cracks called transform faults.

THE EARTH'S CHANGING FACE

A space traveller passing the Earth 200 million years ago would have seen one large landmass and one vast blue ocean. But around 135 million years ago, the landmass, called Pangaea, had started to break up and the pieces were slowly drifting apart. The modern oceans were created between them. Some plates were large. Others, like the one carrying what is now India, were smaller. The Indian plate had been attached to Africa. But around 50 million years ago, it was pushing against the large Eurasian plate. Between the two plates was an ancient ocean. The rocks formed from sediments piled up on the bed of the ocean were squeezed up into the Himalayas, which form the world's highest mountain range.

Above: Plates move past each other like two blocks of wood being pushed in opposite directions. But the movement is not smooth. The plate edges are jagged and the plates are usually locked together. But pressure finally breaks the locks. The plates then move suddenly in a violent jerk.

Right: The map shows the plates into which the Earth's surface is divided. The plates are all moving very slowly. The movements cause earthquakes, volcanic eruptions and the creation of mountain ranges.

Ocean Ridges and Trenches

The study of the oceans in recent years has helped to explain how continents move. No rocks in the oceanic crust are much older than 200 million years. This shows that the oceans are young features, unlike the continents, which have rocks dating back 3800 million years. The youngest rocks are in the middle of long, mostly underwater mountain ranges, or ocean ridges. The rocks in the crust become progressively older away from the ridges in both directions. The ocean ridges are earthquake zones. Earthquakes also occur along the deep ocean trenches, near the edges of the oceans.

Moving Plates

Boundaries between large blocks in the Earth's surface, called plates, run through the ocean ridges. Plates consist of the thin crust, including the continents, and part of the upper mantle. Under the ridges, hot fluid material is rising in the mantle and spreading sideways beneath the plates. These movements are pulling the plates apart by 1 to 10 cm a year. When the plates move, molten material rises to plug the gaps. It then hardens into new crustal rock.

Along the ocean trenches, however, plates are colliding and one plate is being pushed down beneath another. As it descends, the front edge of the plate is melted. Some plates move apart and some collide with each other. A third kind of movement occurs when plates move alongside each other. They move along long cracks in the surface, called transform faults.

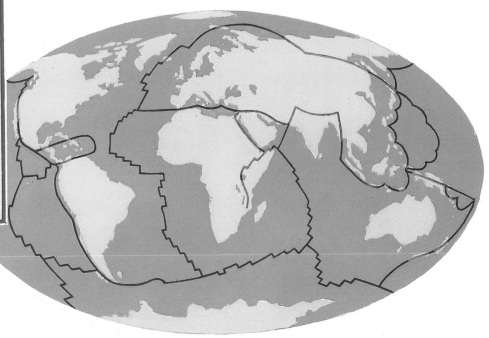

Rocks of the Earth

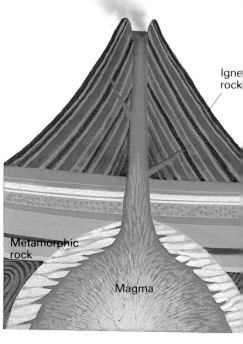

Rocks consist of minerals and most rocks contain several minerals. There are three kinds of rocks: igneous rocks, metamorphic rocks and sedimentary rocks.

Igneous Rocks

The term igneous comes from a Latin word meaning 'fire', and all igneous rocks are formed from hot magma. When magma cools slowly underground, coarse-grained igneous rocks are formed. The grains (or mineral crystals) in the rock are visible with the naked eye. The commonest igneous rock formed in this way is granite.

Other igneous rocks form when magma cools quickly in the air or in water. Fast cooling prevents the formation of crystals and so these rocks are fine-grained. To see the minerals in fine-grained rocks, you must study them through a microscope. The commonest fine-grained igneous rock is basalt.

Metamorphic Rocks

When magma rises upwards, it heats the other rocks. Heat changes rocks, just as wet dough is turned into bread in a hot oven. Rocks are also changed by pressure and by chemical action caused by hot steam and liquids.

Rocks changed by heat, pressure or steam are called metamorphic rocks. The hard metamorphic rock slate (used for roofing) was formerly the soft rock shale or mudstone.

Below: The Grand Canyon is one of the most impressive sights in the world. This vast gorge in Arizona, USA, was cut out by the Colorado river, and in places it reaches a depth of more than 1.5 km. The successive layers of different coloured rocks give its steep walls a striped effect.

Marble is a metamorphic rock formed from limestone. Other metamorphic rocks include gneiss, hornfels and quartzite.

Sedimentary Rocks

Igneous and metamorphic rocks make up 95 per cent of the rocks in the top 16 km of the Earth's crust. But sedimentary rocks cover 75 per cent of the Earth's land surface.

Many sedimentary rocks consist of worn fragments of other rocks. These fragments are piled up, usually in water, and pressed into layers. The loose grains are later cemented together by minerals deposited from seeping water. Such rocks include sandstone and shale. Some sedimentary rocks are deposited from water. They include flint, rock salt and some kinds of limestone. Other limestones consist largely of the remains of dead sea creatures. Coal is another sedimentary rock. It consists of the remains of ancient plants.

Sedimentary rock

Metamorphic rock

Rock fragments

Igneous rock

Above: The diagram shows the main kinds of rock. Igneous rocks are formed when molten magma is pushed upwards through the Earth's crust and cools and hardens. Some magma reaches the surface and some cools underground. Metamorphic rocks are rocks that have been changed by great heat or by pressure. The third type is called sedimentary rock. Many sedimentary rocks are formed from fragments of sand, mud or the remains of dead sea creatures which pile up in water.

Mountains

The four main kinds of mountains are fold mountains, block mountains and volcanic and dome mountains.

Fold Mountains

Folds are bends in layers of rock caused by sideways movements in the Earth's crust. Upfolds are called anticlines and downfolds are called synclines.

Fold mountains rise when two plates in the Earth's crust push against each other. Flat layers of rock between the plates are then buckled upwards into huge loops. For example, the Himalayas are fold mountains caused by a collision between a plate bearing India and another plate bearing the rest of Asia (see pages 10-11). The Alps started to rise when, about 26 million years ago, the African plate pushed a small plate bearing Italy against the underside of Europe.

Block Mountains

When plates move, they crack nearby rocks. Long cracks are called faults. Plate movements cause faults to open up and push the cracked rocks up and down along the faults. Large blocks of land squeezed upwards along faults are called horsts or block mountains.

Volcanic and Dome Mountains

Volcanic mountains are made up of erupted magma. Sometimes magma rises upwards but does not reach the surface. It pushes the overlying rocks up into domes. When the overlying rocks are worn away, the hardened magma is exposed as a dome mountain.

Fold mountains are formed by lateral (sideways) pressure. Flat layers of rock are arched up into folds. Fold mountain ranges include the Himalayas in Asia, the Alps in Europe, the Rockies in North America and the Andes in South America

14

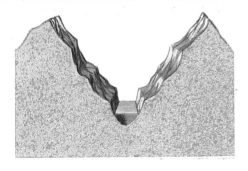

Fast-flowing rivers in mountainous regions wear out deep, V-shaped valleys.

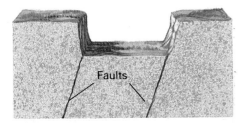

Faults

Rift valleys form when blocks of land sink downwards between two sets of faults.

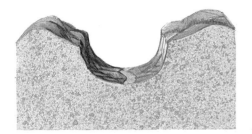

Steep-sided U-shaped valleys are worn out by glaciers (tongues of ice) in mountain regions.

Valleys and Slopes

Even as mountains are pushed upwards, so the forces of erosion start to wear them down. Weathering breaks up rocks. Rivers and glaciers carry worn material away. In doing so, they wear out deep valleys. Rift valleys are not eroded. They are formed when blocks of land slip down between faults.

Steep slopes are the main feature of mountain areas. Rocks on steep slopes are unstable. They may be dislodged by earthquakes to cause landslides, earth flows (movements of fine soil and clay), mud flows (made of dust and sand or volcanic ash mixed with water), and avalanches (falls of ice, snow and rock).

Landslides are movements of soil and rock down a cliff or mountainside. Landslides can do much damage and cause loss of life.

KINDS OF MOUNTAINS

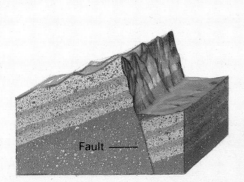

Fault

Block mountains are formed when a large block of land is pushed upwards along a fault (crack) or between two faults in the Earth's crust. The Sierra Nevada range in California in the south-western United States is an example of a block mountain.

Some volcanic mountains consist of volcanic ash and other fragments of magma which have been exploded into the air. Others are huge piles of hardened lava. Most volcanoes contain layers of ash alternating with layers of lava.

LANDSLIDES AND AVALANCHES

Some of the most destructive landslides and avalanches are caused by earthquakes.

For example, an earthquake in 1840 caused a landslide in the Himalayas. Rocks crashed down a gorge into the Indus River. The rocks dammed the river and a 64-km long lake formed behind the rocks. When the dam burst, a flood destroyed everything in its path for hundreds of kilometres downstream.

A landslide in Italy in 1963 sent many rocks crashing into a man-made lake. Water surged over the dam, wiping out the resort of Longarone.

In 1970, an avalanche in Peru killed 18,000 people.

Volcanoes

Volcanoes are vents (holes) in the ground where magma reaches the Earth's surface. The magma may appear in flows of molten lava or as fragments, including volcanic ash and sizeable volcanic bombs. Mountains built of magma are also called volcanoes.

There are more than 500 active volcanoes. Active volcanoes have erupted in historic times. Between eruptions, they are dormant (sleeping). Volcanoes that are unlikely to erupt again are extinct.

Where Volcanoes Occur

Most volcanoes lie near the edges of the moving plates in the Earth's crust (see pages 10-11). Some are on the ocean ridges. Others are near places where one plate is descending beneath another. The descending plate is melted to produce magma. A few volcanoes, like those in Hawaii, lie far from plate edges. They are probably above hot spots in the Earth's mantle.

Right: This diagram of a volcano shows that magma rises from an underground chamber (1) to the crater (2) during eruptions. Ash is sometimes exploded into the air while lava (3) flows from the crater. The ash and lava pile up to form a volcanic mountain. Sheets of magma are forced into nearby rocks. Some called dykes (4) cut across existing layers, while sills (5) run between existing layers. Some magma may be forced through secondary vents (6) in the side of the mountain. Runny lava may rise through long faults (7) and spread out over the land. Extinct volcanoes (8) have not erupted in historic times. Magma heats water in the rocks. Some water appears in hot springs and geysers (9), which are high jets of hot water and steam.

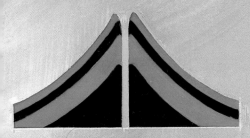

Volcanoes formed from ash and cinder are steep-sided. Cones like these often build up inside craters between major eruptions.

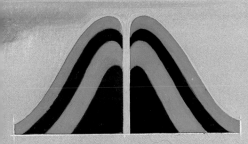

Thick, pasty lava flows only a short distance before it hardens. It also forms volcanic mountains with steep slopes.

Runny lava flows great distances. As a result, it forms flattened volcanoes, like upturned saucers, as in Hawaii.

Kinds of Volcanoes

Some volcanoes erupt in huge explosions. These volcanoes contain pasty magma. Lots of gases and steam are trapped in the magma. The vent of the volcano is usually blocked by a hard plug of magma. Below, the magma is pushing upwards until the pressure becomes so great that the plug is removed. Hot gases and steam then surge from the vent, often followed by a dark cloud of hot ash which races down the mountainside. Huge columns of ash are hurled into the air.

Quiet volcanoes, by contrast, usually contain runny magma, from which gases and steam can easily escape. They do not erupt in great explosions. Instead, they emit long streams of fluid lava. However, most volcanoes are intermediate in type. They sometimes erupt explosively and sometimes quietly.

Predicting Eruptions

Scientists keep watch on many active volcanoes. They look out for small earthquakes, swellings in the sides of the mountains and increases in temperatures and pressure. When they think an eruption is likely, they warn people and ask them to leave the area.

GREAT VOLCANIC ERUPTIONS

GREATEST VOLCANIC EXPLOSION: A volcano on the Greek island of Thera (Santorini) exploded in about 1470 BC with the power of about 130 times the greatest H-bomb detonation.
GREATEST MODERN EXPLOSION: People 4700 km away heard the volcanic explosion on the Indonesian island of Krakatoa in 1883. But this explosion was probably only about one-fifth as powerful as that at Thera.
GREATEST ERUPTION: Tambora, a volcano on the Indonesian island of Sumbawa, erupted in 1815. It was the greatest in terms of the amount of rock removed. The total amount of rock exploded away was probably two and a half to three times as much as at Thera.

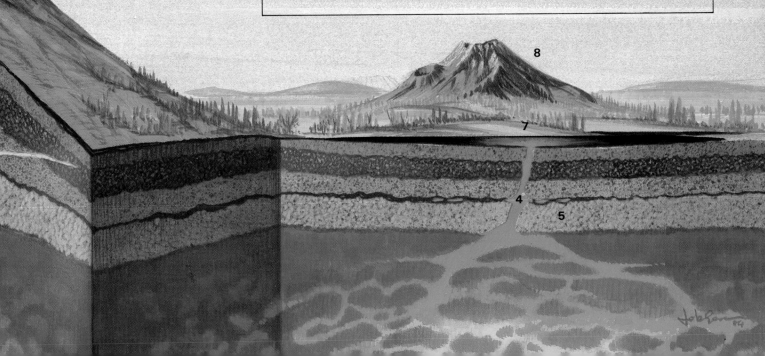

Earthquakes

The Trembling Earth

Earthquakes can occur anywhere. They may be caused by landslides or by volcanic eruptions. But most are caused by movements along faults in rocks which shake the land. Most do little or no damage. But a few earthquakes cause great destruction.

The place inside the Earth where an earthquake occurs is called the focus. The most destructive earthquakes have a focus that is within about 60 km of the surface. Earth movements at much deeper levels have less effect at the surface. The point on the surface above the focus is called the epicentre. The epicentres of many earthquakes are in the oceans. The tremors may set off fast moving waves called tsunamis. Tsunamis can cause great damage far away from the epicentre.

Below: The map shows that most earthquakes occur in clearly defined zones. Earthquakes can occur anywhere, but most of them, including the most intense, are concentrated around the edges of the moving plates into which the Earth's crust is divided.

Bottom: During severe earthquakes, like the one that hit Anchorage and other towns in Alaska in 1964, large cracks may open up in the shaking ground. Buildings collapse and landslides often cause great damage. Other hazards include fires, which often do even more damage than the earthquake, and tsunamis (high waves) that strike coastal areas, sweeping ships inland.

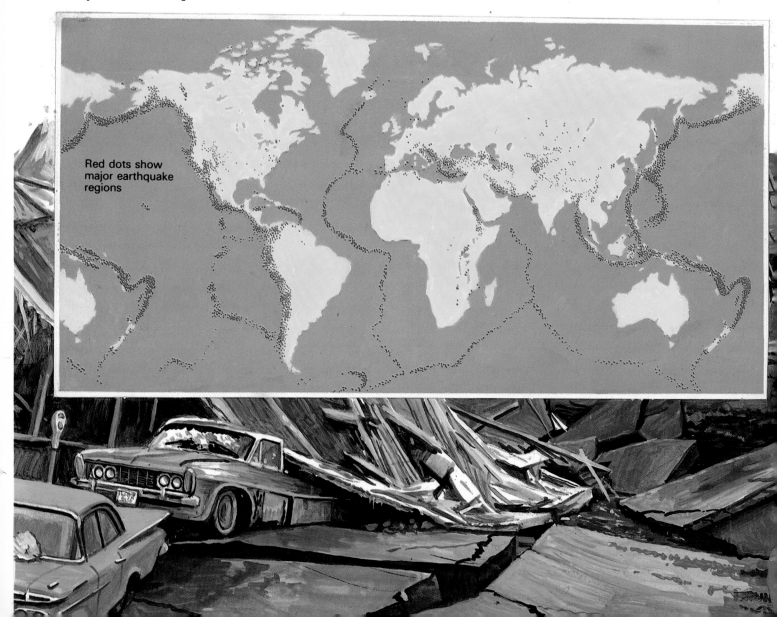

Red dots show major earthquake regions

Where Earthquakes Occur

The chief earthquake zones follow the edges of the plates in the Earth's crust, namely the ocean ridges, zones where one plate is descending beneath another, and transform faults. Earthquakes occur when plates move in sudden jerks. The San Andreas (transform) fault runs through California, in the south-western USA. A movement along this fault in 1906 shook the city of San Francisco. Fires destroyed much property. Since 1906, scientists have found ways of building houses that will not collapse during 'quakes.

Earthquake Prediction

Scientists want to find ways of predicting earthquakes. They have discovered that rocks may be deformed as pressure builds up before a 'quake. Other changes in rocks and even unusual behaviour by animals, which seem to sense danger, are also being studied. But earthquake forecasting is still a young science.

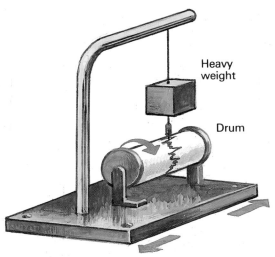

Heavy weight

Drum

Above: Seismographs are sensitive instruments used to record earthquakes. When an earthquake occurs, the heavy weight suspended from the frame stays almost still while the support shakes. The vibrations are recorded on a piece of paper wrapped around a slowly revolving drum.

The Work of Rivers

Running water is a major force in shaping the land. In itself, water has little power to erode (wear away) rock. But rivers push loose boulders, stones and sand along their courses. As they do so, the loose material scrapes the river bed and loosens other rocks. In this way, rivers can wear out deep valleys. River water also dissolves some rocks. Of all the material carried by rivers, about 30 per cent is dissolved rock and 70 per cent is solid material. Most rivers can be divided into three distinctive stages. They are called youth, maturity and old age.

Above: Youthful rivers rise in glaciers, lakes or springs. They flow swiftly downhill and wear out deep V-shaped valleys. Erosion occurs when the river is in flood.

Youthful Rivers

Rivers originate in several ways. Some flow from melting glaciers. Some drain out of lakes. Others start in springs where water bubbles to the surface.

In mountain areas, youthful rivers flow rapidly straight down steep slopes. After rains or when snow melts in spring, they become raging torrents. They then wear away their beds and carve out deep, V-shaped valleys.

Above: In middle age, rivers develop meanders (bends) and so lateral (sideways) erosion becomes more important than downward erosion. As a result, the valleys become broader and broader.

Right: The diagram shows features of a river in old age. On straight stretches, the channel is symmetrical (1). On bends, the outer bend is undercut, but sediment is dumped on the inner bend (2). In old age, when a river floods, particles are dumped on the river banks to form mounds called levees (3). Other features are oxbow lakes (abandoned meanders) and deltas where the river divides into channels.

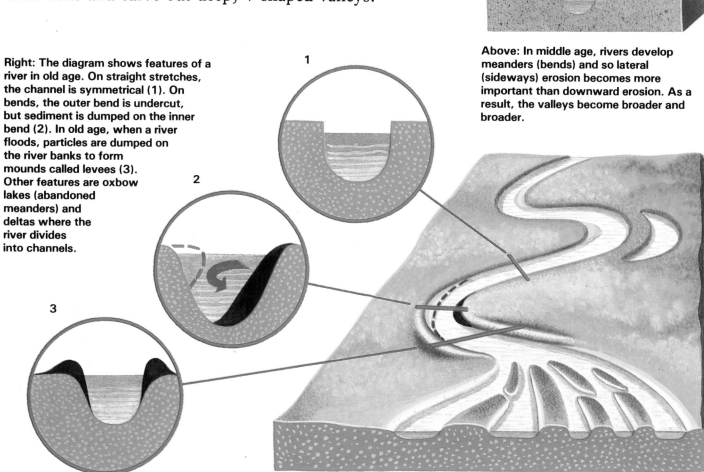

Mature Rivers

When rivers emerge from mountains, they slow down as they flow over less steep slopes. They develop large, sweeping bends, called meanders. Mature rivers do not deepen their valleys like youthful rivers. But the strong currents constantly widen the valleys.

Old Age Rivers

In old age, rivers flow slowly across nearly flat plains. There is little erosion, although the rivers carry huge amounts of fine sediment. When the rivers overflow, the sediment is spread over the land. Large particles are dropped on the river banks, where they pile up to form mounds called levees. Fine particles are swept long distances from the river.

In old age, rivers sometimes change course. They cut through the necks of bends and so straighten their courses. The bends then become 'abandoned meanders', or oxbow lakes, which later dry up. Some rivers dump much of their load of sediment at their mouths in areas called deltas. But in places where tidal currents are strong, the sediment is swept out to sea.

WATERFALLS

Many waterfalls, including Niagara Falls in North America, occur where rivers flow over hard rocks that resist erosion. The diagram, above, shows a waterfall of this kind. The softer rocks below are undercut so that, occasionally, parts of the overlying rock break off and crash down. Such falls gradually retreat upstream. On average, Niagara Falls is retreating by about 0.9 metres a year.

Other falls occur along steep escarpments that separate highlands from lowlands. Others occur in glaciated regions, where rivers plunge into deep U-shaped valleys.

The world's highest waterfall is Angel Falls, Venezuela. It is 979 metres high.

Shaping the Land

Right: Limestone caves are worn out by rainwater. Limestone consists mostly of calcium carbonate. This substance reacts chemically with rainwater, which eats away the rock along the horizontal and vertical cracks in the rock. Water seeping through the caves is highly charged with calcium carbonate.
Water dripping from the roof of a cave is often agitated and evaporated by air currents. Thin films of the mineral calcite are then deposited from the water. Layer upon layer of such deposits build downwards to form the icicle-like stalactites. Water splashing onto the floor of a cave also deposits calcite. These build upwards into stalagmites.

Although it is difficult to see, the land in your home area is slowly changing. American scientists have worked out that about 0.3 metres of land is removed from the eastern USA every 9000 years. This may not seem much. But if you remember that we measure Earth history in millions of years, you will realize that mountains can be worn down to plains. The main forces that shape the land are weathering, winds, rivers, ice and, along coasts, sea waves.

Weathering occurs in several ways. For example, rain is important, because some minerals, such as rock salt, dissolve in water. Some rocks, such as limestones, do not dissolve in pure water. But limestone dissolves in water which contains carbon dioxide dissolved from the air or soil. The dissolved gas changes the water into a weak acid. This acid wears out limestone caves.

Rainwater also affects the hard rock granite. This is because water combines with some kinds of feldspar and turns them into clay. The quartz and mica in granite are not affected. Grains of these minerals are washed away by rain and rivers. The quartz grains often form sandy beaches along coasts.

Above: Plants contribute to the break-up of rocks. Here, a seedling has taken root in a crack in a boulder. As the tree grows, the roots exert great pressure, pushing the boulder apart.

Weathering in Mountains and Deserts

In mountain areas, water seeps into cracks in rocks during the day. At night, temperatures often fall below zero and the water freezes. Ice occupies nine per cent more space than the same amount of water and so, when water freezes, it expands and the ice pushes against the sides of cracks. When this happens night after night, the cracks are widened and the rocks are finally split apart. This is called frost action. The shattered rocks tumble downhill. They often pile up in heaps called talus or scree.

In deserts, rocks are heated by the Sun by day. In the evening, temperatures fall quickly, often to below freezing point. The fast cooling of the rocks cracks the surfaces, making sounds like pistol shots. Layers of rock then peel away.

Sand covers about one-fifth of the world's deserts. Winds blow the grains of sand around, piling them up into hills called dunes. Dunes move in the direction of the prevailing (usual) wind. Grains of sand are blown up the gentle windward slopes and then topple down the steep slip faces. In this way, the dune slowly advances from position 1 to 2, 3, 4, 5 and so on.

Plants and Animals

As shown in the picture on the facing page, the roots of trees and shrubs can split rocks apart and so they also contribute to weathering. But plants also protect the land, especially when grass roots bind loose soil particles together.

Worms, which eat vast amounts of soil, and burrowing animals, such as rodents and termites, also play their part, because churned up soil is easily removed by rain and wind.

Right: Many desert features were carved by water at times in the past when the desert had a moist climate. Today, wind-blown sand eats away rocks along lines of weakness and polishes rocks, such as this natural arch.

DESERT LANDSCAPES

There are three main kinds of desert landscapes: sandy deserts called *erg*; stony deserts called *reg*; and bare rocky deserts called *hammada*.

Deserts have little rain, but the main land features in most deserts were carved out by running water at a time when the climate was very different from that of today. Even now, a rare thunderstorm can drown areas which have been dry for years. *Wadis* (dry valleys) fill up with rushing torrents that sweep huge amounts of sand and rock away.

But wind-blown sand is the main natural form of erosion in deserts today. It can strip the paint off cars and undercut telegraph poles and boulders. It is responsible for mushroom-shaped boulders with a large top resting on a narrow stem. Wind-blown sand also grinds out deep hollows in rocky surfaces.

In sandy deserts, the wind blows the sand into dunes. *Barchans* are crescent-shaped dunes, while *seif dunes* are long sand ridges.

The Sea in Motion

The oceans cover about 71 per cent of the Earth's surface. Ocean water is always moving, even in the deepest trenches. We know this because fishes live there. If the water was still, the oxygen dissolved in the water would have been used up long ago.

Winds and Waves

Waves appear to move seawater. In fact, they make water particles rotate, but do not move them forwards. Most waves are caused by winds. Tsunamis are waves generated by earthquakes. These low but fast-moving waves often pass unnoticed in the open sea. But near land, they build up to great heights. A tsunami off Japan reached a height of 85 metres.

High Tide, Low Tide

Tides are caused by the gravitational pull of the Moon and, to a lesser extent, of the Sun. They occur twice every 24 hours and 50 minutes. This is the time taken by the Moon to complete one orbit of the Earth.

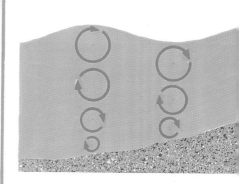

Above: When a wave passes through water, the particles of water rotate in a circular motion, but they are not moved sideways. The wave length is the distance between the crests of two successive waves. Along coasts, there is not enough water to complete the wave and so the wave breaks.

Ships caught at sea during a bad storm run the risk of capsizing. The highest waves in the open sea are caused by strong winds. The highest recorded wave measured 34 metres between the trough and the crest.

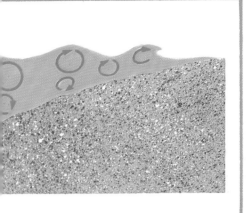

Rivers in the Sea

Sailors are interested in ocean currents, because they affect navigation. These currents, which are caused mainly by prevailing winds, only affect the top 350 metres. Other currents lower down often move in an opposite direction to those on the surface. Many deep-sea currents are caused by variations in the density of the water. These result from differences in salinity (saltness) and temperature. Salty, cold water is denser (heavier) than less salty, warm water.

The circulation of ocean water by currents has an important effect on climate. Warm currents convey heat to cool temperate and polar regions. Cold currents also modify the climate of tropical regions.

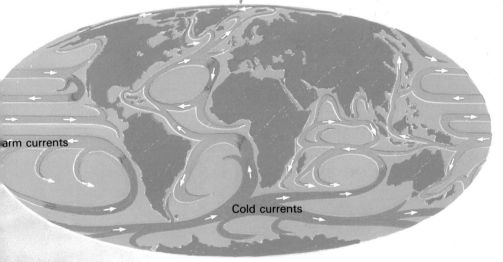

arm currents

Cold currents

OCEAN CURRENTS

Ocean currents ensure that seawater is always on the move. The currents on the map (left) are caused mainly by winds. Ocean currents flow at 1-5 knots and so are important in navigation. Slower currents are called drifts. The slow northern extension of the fast Gulf Stream is the North Altantic Drift.

Other currents flow at lower levels. For example, warm currents flow towards the polar regions. There, denser (heavier) cold polar water sinks beneath the warm water and flows towards the equator.

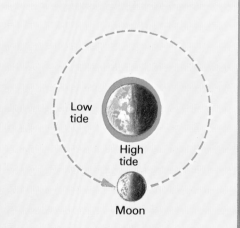

Spring tides

Sun   Moon   Low tide

High tide

Neap tides

Sun

Low tide

High tide

Moon

Tides are caused by the gravitational pull of the Moon and the Sun on the waters of the oceans. The highest tides are called spring tides. They occur when the Sun, Moon and Earth are in a straight line (above). The Moon's and the Sun's gravity are then combined.

The lowest tides are called neap tides. They occur when the Sun, Earth and Moon form a right angle (as shown above). The gravitational pull of the Moon is then opposed by the Sun's gravitational pull. Neap and spring tides each occur twice every month.

Mapping the Land

Maps show the world or parts of it on flat surfaces. Accurate maps are drawn to scale. At a scale of 1:50,000, 1 cm on the map equals 50,000 cm or 0.5 km on the ground.

Surveying the Land

The first job of land surveyors (people who measure the land) is to fix as accurately as possible the positions of a network of points, by measuring the angles and distances between them. Surveyors use telescopic instruments, theodolites, to measure angles. Measuring distances was once a slow process, using metal tapes. But surveyors can now use electronic instruments. When the positions of the points are known, their heights are measured. These fixed points, which are often marked on the ground by concrete pillars, form the skeleton of a map.

MAP SYMBOLS

CONTOURS are lines joining places with the same height. They are usually brown lines, but underwater contours are blue.

CULTURAL FEATURES are man-made things, such as towns, churches, historical sites, including battlefields (crossed swords), lighthouses, roads and railways. They usually appear in red or black.

HACHURES are fine lines that show land forms three-dimensionally.

LAYER TINTING is the use of colours and shades of colours to show the various levels of the land.

SPOT HEIGHTS are black dots or solid black triangles. A figure in metres or feet alongside the point shows the exact height.

VEGETATION FEATURES, such as forests and swamps, are usually depicted as green symbols.

WATER FEATURES, such as rivers, lakes and coasts, are shown in blue.

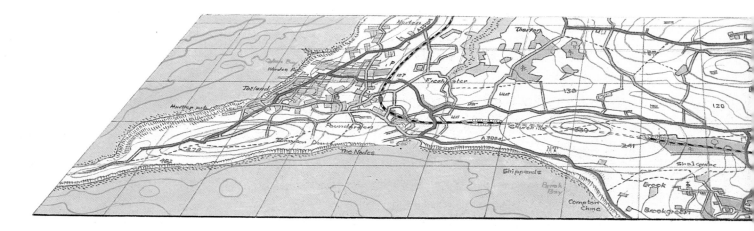

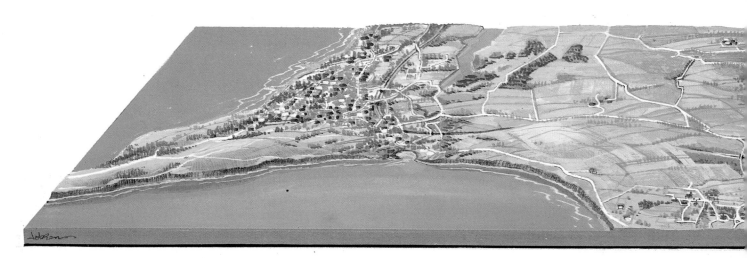

Detailed Mapping

When the network of points is fixed, surveyors must measure all the details of the land between them. This work was once done on the ground. But, today, mapping from air photographs has largely replaced ground mapping.

Aircraft take long strips of photographs of the land. Each photograph overlaps the next by 60 per cent. The fixed ground points are identified on the photographs. Because the distances between them are known, other distances can be measured on the photographs.

Heights can also be measured. This is because overlapping photographs viewed through a stereoscope appear as a three-dimensional model of the land.

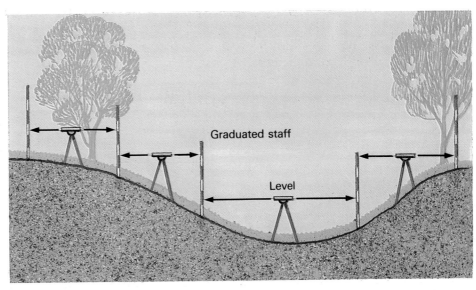

Graduated staff

Level

Above: To fix heights, surveyors use a telescopic instrument called a level, which is mounted on a tripod, and a graduated staff. The difference between the height of the level and a reading on the staff is the height difference between the two points.

Below: Topographic maps, or general reference maps, show the main features of the land over fairly small areas. They are drawn to scale so that any distance on the map represents a distance on the ground. In order to include as many details as possible, map-makers use symbols like those shown below. You will find a legend (key), containing all the symbols used on a map in the margins of most topographic maps.

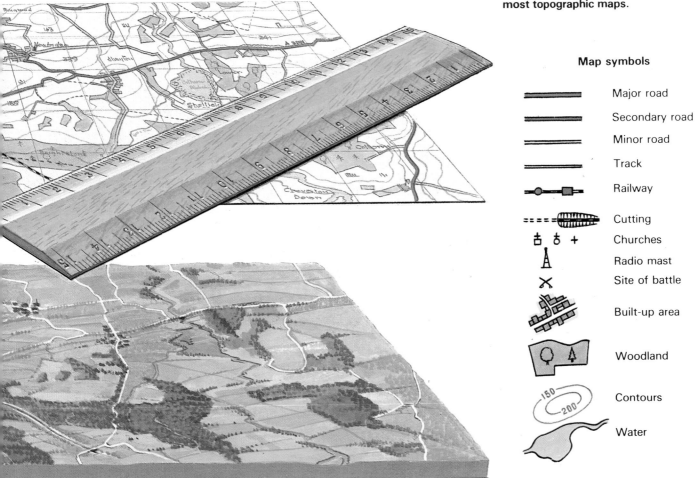

Map symbols

Major road

Secondary road

Minor road

Track

Railway

Cutting

Churches

Radio mast

Site of battle

Built-up area

Woodland

Contours

Water

The World is Round

Geographers are interested in features on the Earth's surface and how the features are related to one another. The best way to present the information which geographers need is a map. The facts on a map would often fill a book.

Types of Maps

Apart from topographic, or general reference, maps, there are many special kinds of maps. For example, weather maps show the weather conditions over a large area, and population maps show where people are most concentrated. Special maps are now often produced by computers. They can be a great help to planners.

Some maps are large-scale, covering small areas. Maps with extremely large scales are called *plans*. But small-scale maps cover large areas. Such maps appear in atlases. Small-scale maps create problems for map-makers.

Curved Surfaces, Flat Maps

A major problem faced by map-makers is that the Earth is nearly a sphere. Its surface is curved, not flat. To understand the problem, think of another sphere, an orange.

If you peel an orange, keeping the peel in one piece, you are left with a hollow sphere. It is impossible to turn this sphere into a flat surface without breaking it and crushing the pieces. To deal with this problem, map-makers have devised various solutions — map projections.

Map Projections

Map projections are ways of *projecting* details on a curved surface onto a flat surface.

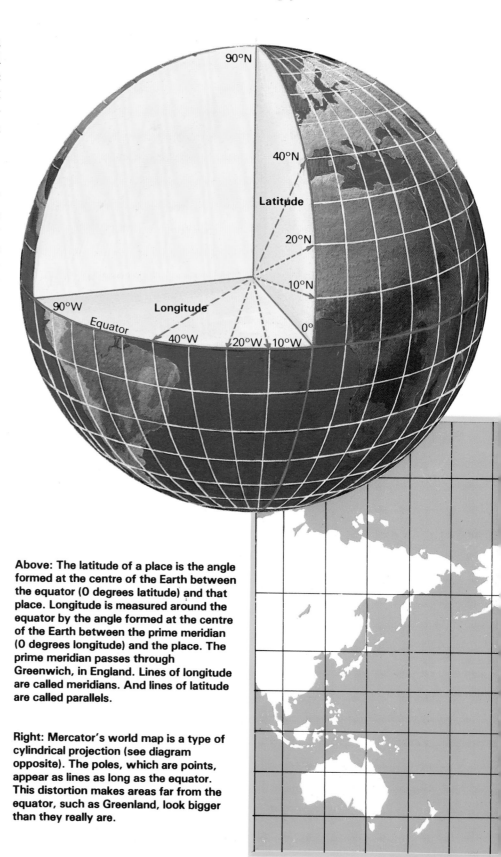

Above: The latitude of a place is the angle formed at the centre of the Earth between the equator (0 degrees latitude) and that place. Longitude is measured around the equator by the angle formed at the centre of the Earth between the prime meridian (0 degrees longitude) and the place. The prime meridian passes through Greenwich, in England. Lines of longitude are called meridians. And lines of latitude are called parallels.

Right: Mercator's world map is a type of cylindrical projection (see diagram opposite). The poles, which are points, appear as lines as long as the equator. This distortion makes areas far from the equator, such as Greenland, look bigger than they really are.

Some projections are devised as though the Earth is a glass sphere with all the details and lines of latitude and longitude engraved on it. If you place a light at the center of the globe, the engraved lines are projected as shadows onto flat surfaces. A cylindrical projection of this type is shown below. But most projections are worked out by mathematics.

No one map can show shapes, areas, distances and directions correctly at the same time. Only a globe can do that. Some map projections preserve some features and some preserve others. Equal area maps, for instance, ensure that all countries are the right *size*. Conformal maps make sure that the *shape* of the countries is correct. The type of projection depends on the purpose of the map.

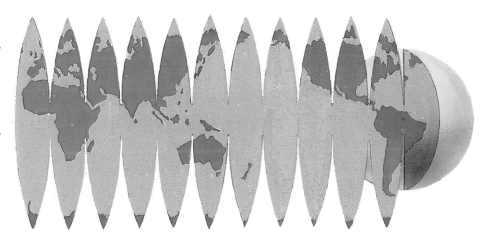

Above: The problem of showing a curved surface on a flat piece of paper is revealed when globes are made. The world map is first printed on a series of thin, lens-shaped pieces of paper, called gores. The gores are fitted together on the globe and pasted down. Some map projections are drawn in separate sections, resembling gores. Such projections are said to be interrupted. Maps based on interrupted projections are of little use, however, because they split up land masses.

Below: Cylindrical map projections are developed as though a light was placed at the center of an engraved glass globe. Around the globe is a cylinder of paper, touching the globe along the equator. The light casts shadows of the engraved meridians and parallels, together with the shapes of the continents, onto the paper. This creates a map. But you can see that the distances between lines of latitude increase towards the poles. On a true map, these distances should be the same.

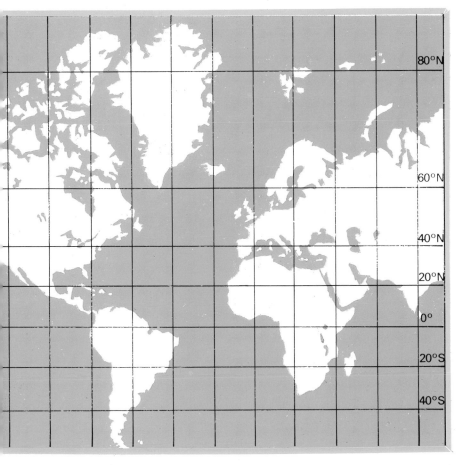

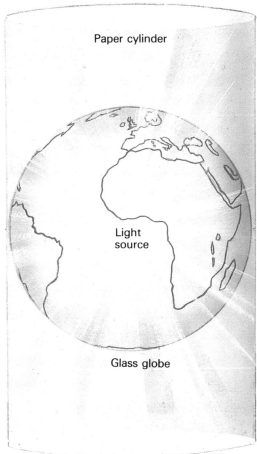

Paper cylinder

Light
source

Glass globe

Cloud, Wind and Rain

Air is always moving because of the Sun's heat. At the equator, hot air rises. This creates a zone of low air pressure at the surface, called the *doldrums*. The rising air eventually cools and spreads out north and south. It finally sinks back to the Earth at around latitude 30° North and 30° South. These are the *horse latitudes*. Regions where air is sinking are high air pressure zones. From the horse latitudes, trade winds blow towards the equator and westerly winds blow towards the poles. From the poles — also high air pressure regions — come the polar easterlies. The trade winds, westerlies and polar easterlies are the prevailing (chief) winds of their various regions.

The Sun evaporates water from the oceans. Warm air can hold more water vapour than cold air. But when warm air rises and cools, it finally reaches *dew point*, when the air contains all the vapour it can at that temperature. More cooling makes water vapour *condense* (liquefy) into water droplets or ice crystals, which form clouds. In clouds, water droplets collide to become raindrops. The ice crystals also grow in size. They fall as snow or, in warm air, as raindrops.

Cirrus (a high cloud) is wispy and made of ice crystals.

Cirrocumulus (a high cloud) is thin with ripples or rounded masses.

Cirrostratus (a high cloud) may cause halos around the Sun or Moon.

Altocumulus (a medium cloud) consists of rounded masses.

Altostratus (a medium cloud) is a greyish sheet cloud.

Cumulus (a low cloud) is a white heap cloud.

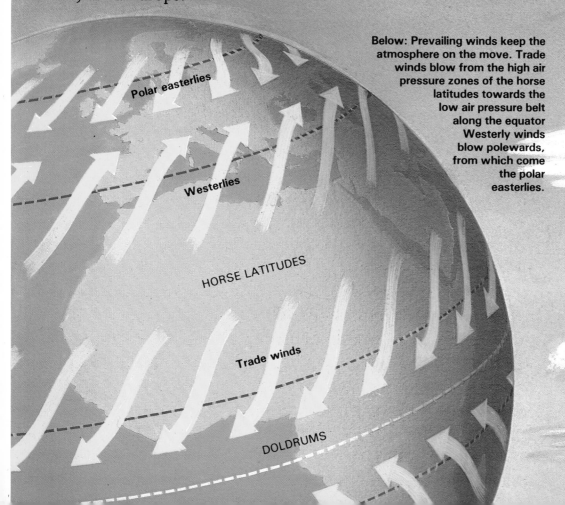

Below: Prevailing winds keep the atmosphere on the move. Trade winds blow from the high air pressure zones of the horse latitudes towards the low air pressure belt along the equator Westerly winds blow polewards, from which come the polar easterlies.

Polar easterlies

Westerlies

HORSE LATITUDES

Trade winds

DOLDRUMS

(1) Orographic rain occurs when winds blow over mountains. The rising air cools, clouds form and rain falls on the windward slopes. Beyond the mountain tops, the air descends and gets warmer, drying the land. This is a rain shadow region.

(2) Convectional rain occurs when the Sun heats the Earth's surface which, in turn, heats the air near the ground. The warm air rises in fast currents. Eventually, the rising air cools, clouds form and rain starts to fall.

(3) Cyclonic rain occurs in depressions (or cyclones) when warm air rises above blocks of cold air.

Cumulonimbus (thundercloud) may extend from 300 to 12,000 metres.

Stratus (a low cloud) is a grey layer cloud.

Climates of the World

The climate is the average, or usual, weather of a place. Climates vary between the poles and the equator.

Climatic Regions

There are six main climatic regions. *Polar climates* are regions where the average temperature in the warmest month is less than 10°C. This is the climate of the frozen wastes around the poles and also the tundra, where the snow melts in summer.

Cold (coniferous) *forest* climates occur in a zone that stretches across North America and Eurasia. The average temperature in the coldest month is less than −3°C. But in the warmest month, the average temperature is above 10°C.

Temperate climates have an average temperature in the coldest month of not less than −3°C, but not more than 18°C. This climate includes mixed forest, deciduous forest and Mediterranean regions.

In *dry climates*, the total average yearly rainfall is less than 250 mm. Deserts may be hot or cold.

Tropical rainy climates have average temperatures in every month that are higher than 18°C. Some places have rain throughout the year. Others have one or two marked dry seasons.

Mountain climates vary as one climbs upwards, because temperatures fall with height. Some mountains on the equator have tropical climates at the bottom and polar climates at their snow-capped tops.

Above: Dense rain forests flourish in tropical rainy climates, where high temperatures and abundant rainfall encourage plant growth. The thickest forests are in regions which have rain throughout the year. Less dense forests grow in monsoon regions which have a marked dry season.

Left: In hot deserts, the only places with water are oases. Many oases are springs or wells which get water from the rocks below. Palm trees grow around them and camels can get much-needed water.

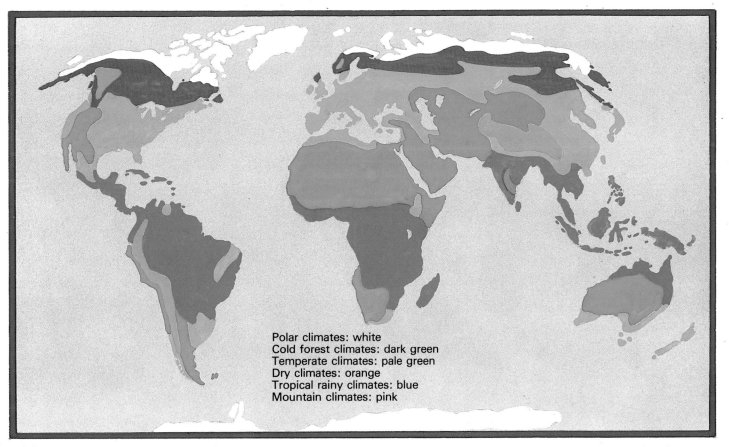

Polar climates: white
Cold forest climates: dark green
Temperate climates: pale green
Dry climates: orange
Tropical rainy climates: blue
Mountain climates: pink

Above: Vast coniferous forests, called taiga, grow in the northern hemisphere in the cold region between the temperate lands to the south and the tree-line, the northernmost limit of tree growth. Birds such as this capercaillie are quite common, though compared with other forests there are few plant and animal species.

Above: The temperate regions of the world were once covered by deciduous trees, which shed their leaves in winter. But most of the trees have now been cut down and replaced by farmland.

Top: The map shows the major climatic regions of the world.

Above: Around the poles, ice and snow blanket the land all the year round. But in the northern hemisphere, between the lands of permanent ice and the tree-line, is a zone called the tundra. This zone comes alive during the short, warm summer when the snow melts. Animal migrants such as musk-oxen and reindeer graze on the tundra. And the arctic fox's white coat turns red during the short summer months.

Industry

Industry Around the World
In the last 200 years, the economies of many countries have changed, as farming and small-scale craft industries have become less important than mining and large-scale factory production. Such countries have been *industrialized*. The Industrial Revolution began in Britain in the late 18th century and Belgium, France, Germany and the USA soon followed. In the late 19th century, other countries, such as Canada, Japan, Russia and Sweden also began to industrialize.

The Pattern of Industry
The industrialized world now includes most of North America, Europe, the USSR, Japan, Australia and New Zealand. But most of Central and South America, Africa and Asia have not been industrialized, although some countries, such as Brazil and China, already have sizeable industries which are expected to expand rapidly in the near future. Many poor countries would like to industrialize, but they lack the money and skilled workers needed to found industries.

Light and Heavy Industry
Light industry produces a wide range of goods, which are generally smaller than those produced by heavy industry. For example, the many consumer products which we find in supermarkets, including clothes, foods and household goods, are produced by light industries. Light industries are now changing because of the introduction of computers and automation.

Heavy industry is associated with huge factories, which use bulky raw materials to produce heavy products. Examples include the iron and steel industry, the chemical industry and heavy engineering, such as shipbuilding. Heavy industries were once located on coal- or iron-fields, because this reduced the cost of transporting these heavy raw materials. But many industries which use oil have spread to other areas in recent years. This is because oil is easily transported through pipelines.

Some industries are neither light nor heavy. For example, car assembly and aerospace industries combine elements from both.

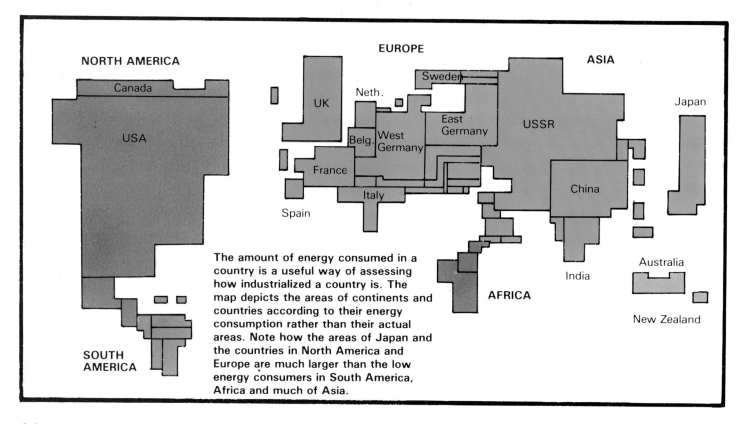

The amount of energy consumed in a country is a useful way of assessing how industrialized a country is. The map depicts the areas of continents and countries according to their energy consumption rather than their actual areas. Note how the areas of Japan and the countries in North America and Europe are much larger than the low energy consumers in South America, Africa and much of Asia.

Steel is the most important material used in shipbuilding, one of the world's leading heavy industries. In recent years, shipbuilders have made larger ships, including vast oil tankers, which can carry large amounts of bulk freight. Europe was once the main centre of shipbuilding. But by the early 1980s Japan led the world, producing 48% of the world's merchant vessels. At the end of the 1980s Japan was still the world's biggest producer of merchant ships, making 37% of the world's output. South Korea was in second place with 29%. Following these two countries were West Germany and Taiwan.

Farming Round the World

Some countries are densely populated, but have only a small area of flat farmland. They build terraces, like a series of steps, down hillsides. The walls around the terraces stop rainwater running downwards washing away the soil.

The world's chief farming nations are China, the USSR, the USA and India. But their farming industries differ greatly. In the USSR and the USA, farmers use modern machinery and yields are high. In China and India, much of the work is done by hand and yields are lower.

There are two main types of farming. Arable farming is the growing of crops. Pastoral farming is the production of meat and other animal products.

Tropical Farming

Many farmers in the tropics are poor, producing only enough food for their families. This is subsistence farming. Some farmers move every few years, whenever the fertility of their farms is exhausted. Nomadic pastoralists wander around with their animals. These simple forms of farming contrast with tropical plantation agriculture, which uses scientific methods to produce such cash crops as cocoa, coffee and tea.

THE INVENTION OF FARMING

Farming was invented about 10,000 years ago, when people learned how to plant seeds. The earliest known farms were in south-western Asia, but farming began soon afterwards in many other parts of the world. In a short time, most people gave up the old hunting and gathering way of life and settled down to become farmers. The farmers founded the first villages and towns.

In the Nile valley in Egypt, in the Tigris and Euphrates valleys in what is now Iraq, and in the Indus valley of Pakistan, people learned how to irrigate the valleys by moving water from the rivers to their fields. From about 5000 years ago, these valleys became centres of brilliant early civilizations.

ANIMAL FARMING

Domesticated animals such as cattle, sheep, goats, pigs and chickens supply high quality protein in the form of milk or meat. They also provide wool, and hides for leather. More importantly in the developing countries cattle, such as oxen and buffalo, also provide power.

Traditionally farm animals feed by grazing, often using land that is unsuitable for crop cultivation. Nowadays in the West many animals are factory farmed. They are housed in special units and fed on manufactured foods.

Farming in Temperate Lands

Farms near cities in temperate countries produce fresh food for city-dwellers. These farms are called market gardens (truck farms in the USA). This is a type of intensive farming. Intensive farming is important in densely populated countries. By contrast, ranching is a kind of extensive farming. Extensive farms are usually on land which is unsuitable for intensive crop growing. Another type of farming is called mixed farming. Mixed farms produce crops and animal products.

Working Together

In some countries, groups of farmers choose to work together through co-operatives. On co-operatives farmers work together, and share the produce. Collective farms in many communist countries, such as the *sovkhozy* (government-owned farms) in the USSR, are similar except that people here work for a wage.

Below: In developing countries, ancient farming methods survive. Here, an Archimedes screw is used to extract water from the River Nile to irrigate farmland.

Forestry

Wood is a valuable product. It is used in buildings, furniture, paper making and as a fuel. It also has many less obvious uses, as in the manufacture of such things as explosives, manmade fibres and medicines.

Forests cover about one-third of the world's surface. The *coniferous* (evergreen) *forests* are most widespread in the northern hemisphere. They contain cedars, firs, pines and spruces that are adapted to survive long, cold winters. These commercially valuable trees are also called *softwoods*, because most species are easy to saw. The leading softwood producers are the USSR, the USA and Canada.

Temperate hardwood forests contain such deciduous trees as ash, beech, chestnut, elm, hickory, oak and willow, which shed their leaves in autumn. A third type of forest is

In North America, northern Europe and the USSR, forestry is highly mechanized. Lumberjacks fell trees with powersaws and felling machines. Many of the trunks are transported from the logging camps to rivers, where they are floated downstream to a sawmill. Some heavy hardwoods will not float. They must be transported by road or rail.

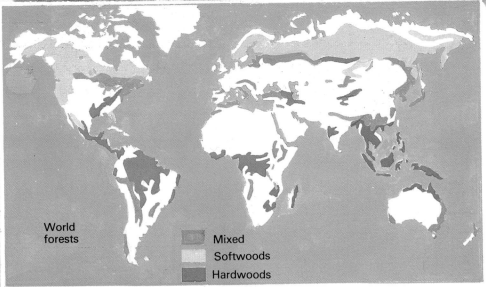

World
forests

Mixed
Softwoods
Hardwoods

Above: The most valuable tropical hardwoods are usually scattered throughout the dense forests. This makes their extraction difficult. In southern Asia elephants are often used to drag the tree trunks through the forest to rivers or loading sites.

Left: The map shows that the world's main softwood forests are in the northern hemisphere — in North America, Scandinavia and the USSR. In some areas, these forests merge southwards into mixed forests and, eventually, deciduous (hardwood) forests. The largest hardwood forests, however, are in the tropics, especially the Amazon basin, central Africa and South-East Asia.

the *mixed forest* zone between the coniferous and hardwood forests. The fourth type of forest, the tropical hardwood forest, contains such trees as ebony, mahogany and teak.

Foresters in the northern coniferous forests replace the trees they cut down with young saplings. However, in recent years, acid rain has been killing many trees. Acid rain is formed when raindrops dissolve harmful gases emitted from factories and power stations.

The huge tropical hardwood forests are being destroyed even faster. The trees are cut down and burnt, to create grazing space for cattle, or for farming. However once the land is cleared the soil rapidly deteriorates and becomes unsuitable for farming or grazing, and another area of forest must be cut down. Every year an area of tropical forest the size of England is destroyed.

Harvest of the Sea

Fish is a valuable food. In some countries, including Japan and Norway, it makes up about one-tenth of people's diets. Freshwater fish form about one-tenth of the world's total catch of 75 million tonnes. The richest ocean fishing grounds are in the north-western Pacific Ocean and in the north-eastern Atlantic Ocean. More fish are caught in the shallow waters of the continental shelves than in the deep ocean waters.

Traditionally, fishermen were hunters, who were never sure of a good catch. Today, however, modern technology is aiding fishermen. For example, radar and sonic depth finders are used to locate shoals of fish.

The use of modern methods has led to overfishing in some areas. This had led to a search for new food products from the oceans. For example, krill, a shrimp-like creature, is found in great quantities around Antarctica. It could be harvested as a food for human consumption, but care must be taken that this does not create a deficit for the seabirds, seals and whales that rely on it as their major food source.

WHALING

For centuries whales have been hunted for their meat, bone and blubber, their huge bodies providing the material for an assortment of goods, ranging from lipstick to fishing rods, shoes to cooking fat. As one species of whale became harder to find because it was over-hunted, and becoming extinct, another, more abundant species would be hunted, so that one type of whale after another became almost extinct.

As early as the 1930s attempts were made to regulate the number of whales killed for commercial use, but it was not until the late 1970s that these regulations were strictly enforced, due to a massive "Save the Whale" campaign. All the products that had been obtained from whales could now be procured from other sources.

Throughout the 1980s some countries ignored the world ban, but nowadays fewer whales are killed for commercial reasons.

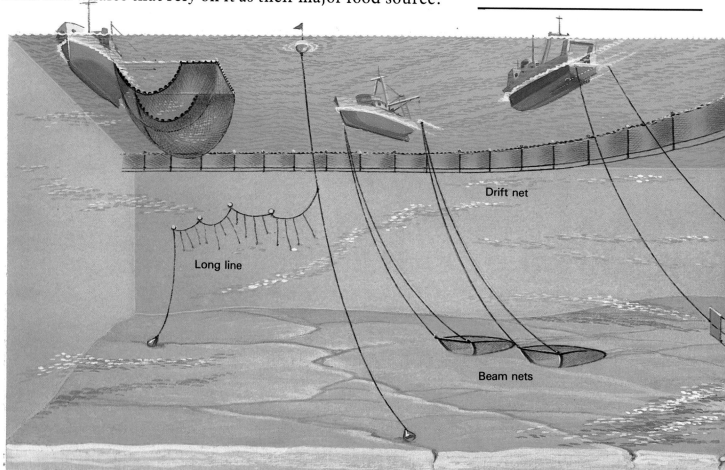

Drift net

Long line

Beam nets

Fish Farming

Attempts are now being made to conserve fish and to develop fish farms. The breeding and raising of fish in tanks and ponds is called aquaculture. Carp have been raised in China for thousands of years, and oysters have been bred in Europe since Roman times.

Today, many species of freshwater fish, including carp, eels and trout are successfully raised. And young salmon are reared in fresh water and later moved to salt water. This mimics the conditions experienced by wild salmon which migrate from rivers to the oceans. The farming of saltwater fish is generally less economic, but overfishing in the oceans is making scientists study saltwater fish farming.

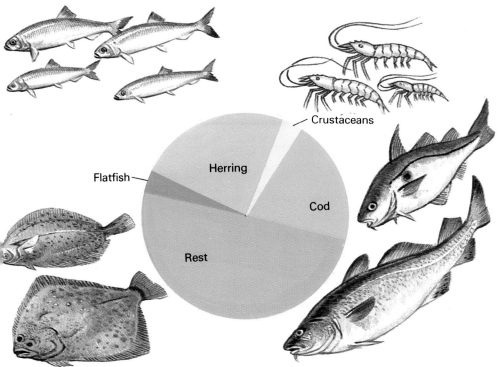

Above: The diagram shows the proportions of various fishes and crustaceans caught around the world. The chief fishing nation is Japan. It accounts for about one-seventh of the world's total catch.

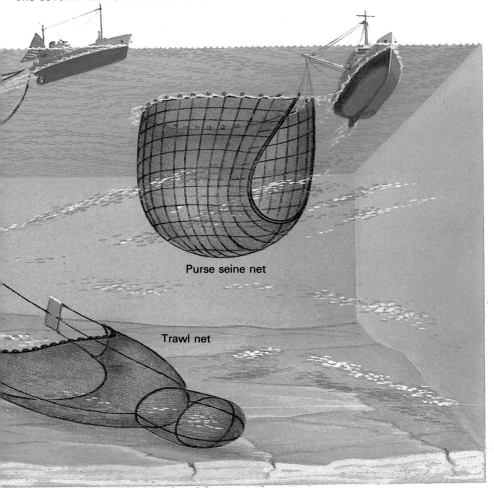

Left: The diagram shows various techniques used in the fishing industry. Long-lining involves putting out long, or ground, lines. Attached to them are short lines with baited hooks. This technique is used to catch tuna.

Drift or gill nets are held up by floats. The gills of fish which try to swim through the nets are caught in the mesh. Many herrings and mackerel are caught by drift nets.

Drag or trawl nets are large, bag-shaped nets which are dragged along the seabed at depths as great as 1000 metres. These nets are used to catch flatfish and other bottom-living fish and crustaceans.

Purse seine nets are used when shoals of such fishes as sardines and herrings are located on the ship's radar. The purse seine nets are then drawn around the shoal.

Pacific shrimp boats haul two beam nets across the sea floor. They catch prawns and shrimps. Many catcher boats now work with a mother factory ship. Instead of returning to port, they deliver their catch to a large factory ship. There the fish are rapidly processed and frozen.

Peoples of the World

People belong to the species *Homo sapiens* (intelligent man). They first appeared around 50,000 years ago. They displaced the closely related Neanderthal people, who died out around the end of the Ice Age.

People vary in appearance. Many of these differences are probably adaptations to the varied climatic conditions in which the people developed. The human family is divided into four main sub-groups: Caucasoids, Mongoloids, Negroids and Australoids.

Caucasoids include the mostly fair-skinned people of Europe and the many people of European origin in other continents. The Arabs of North Africa and most of the much darker skinned people of north-eastern Africa, south-western Asia and India are also Caucasoids.

Mongoloids, with the yellowish skin and straight, dark hair, include most of the people of eastern Asia, Eskimos and American Indians. Negroids include the Black people of Africa and Black Americans, the descendants of Black African slaves.

Australoids include Australian Aborigines, the Veddoids of southern India and the Ainu, the first inhabitants of Japan.

Below: Examples of members of the human family. Most Europeans, Arabs and most people in south-western Asia and India are Caucasoids. Australian Aborigines belong to the Australoid sub-group. The Negroid group includes Black Africans and Black Americans. The Mongoloid sub-group includes most people in eastern Asia and the American Indians. Members of the sub-groups have intermarried. For example, many Mexicans are mestizos, of mixed European and American Indian descent.

Above: The first North Americans came from Asia, perhaps 40,000 years ago, during the Ice Age. The sea level was then much lower than it is today and a land bridge connected northern Asia and North America. These Mongoloid people were the ancestors of the American Indians.

Ways of Life

The ways of life of people still vary greatly around the world. There are still a few people, including the Bushmen and pygmies of Africa, who live much like our ancestors before the invention of agriculture. They live by hunting animals and gathering seeds and roots. Other people are farmers, though many farmers in Africa, Asia and South America are poor. But more and more people are making their homes in cities and towns. Their chief jobs in the developed western countries are in manufacturing and service industries.

Ideas and Beliefs

Different beliefs are important in different places. For some people religion is a very important part of their lives. For others political beliefs, such as communism or socialism, are more important. Whereas in the past there was a tendency to see one's own belief as the only true way of life, nowadays more and more people are tolerant of other people's views, and live in harmony together.

LANGUAGES

There are about 3000 languages and many more dialects. Many have large vocabularies and a written form. Others contain comparatively few words and have no written form.

Some languages are closely related to each other. French, Italian, Portuguese and Spanish all come from Latin, the language of ancient Rome. These languages form the Romance language group. This group belongs to a wider family of languages, called the Indo-European family. This is the world's largest family, followed by the Sino-Tibetan, which includes Chinese.

Some languages have spread around the world. The chief international language is English. French, German and Spanish are also spoken widely throughout the world.

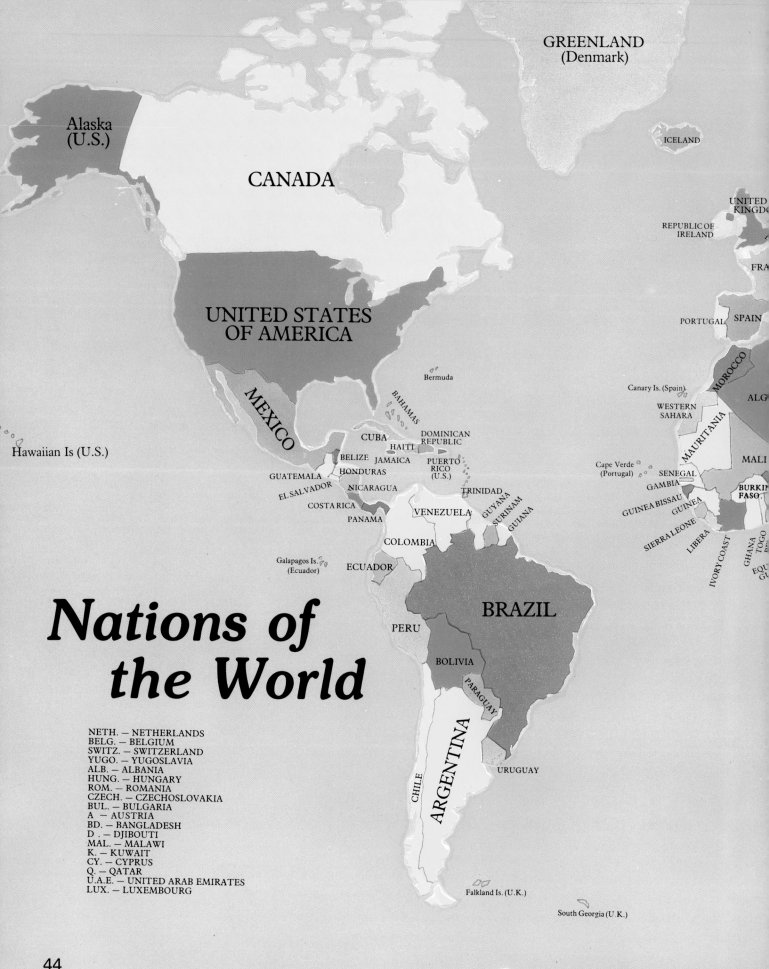

GREENLAND
(Denmark)

ICELAND

Alaska
(U.S.)

CANADA

UNITED
KINGD

REPUBLIC OF
IRELAND

FRA

UNITED STATES
OF AMERICA

PORTUGAL   SPAIN

MOROCCO

Canary Is. (Spain)

ALG

MEXICO

Bermuda

WESTERN
SAHARA

MAURITANIA

MALI

Hawaiian Is (U.S.)

BAHAMAS

CUBA

HAITI

DOMINICAN
REPUBLIC

Cape Verde
(Portugal)

SENEGAL

GAMBIA

BURKIN
FASO.

BELIZE

JAMAICA

PUERTO
RICO
(U.S.)

GUATEMALA   HONDURAS

EL SALVADOR   NICARAGUA

GUINEA BISSAU

GUINEA

SIERRA LEONE

LIBERA

IVORY COAST

GHANA
TOGO

EQU
GU

COSTA RICA

PANAMA

VENEZUELA

TRINIDAD

GUYANA

SURINAM

GUIANA

COLOMBIA

Galapagos Is.
(Ecuador)

ECUADOR

Nations of
the World

PERU

BRAZIL

BOLIVIA

PARAGUAY

CHILE

ARGENTINA

URUGUAY

NETH. — NETHERLANDS
BELG. — BELGIUM
SWITZ. — SWITZERLAND
YUGO. — YUGOSLAVIA
ALB. — ALBANIA
HUNG. — HUNGARY
ROM. — ROMANIA
CZECH. — CZECHOSLOVAKIA
BUL. — BULGARIA
A — AUSTRIA
BD. — BANGLADESH
D . — DJIBOUTI
MAL. — MALAWI
K. — KUWAIT
CY. — CYPRUS
Q. — QATAR
U.A.E. — UNITED ARAB EMIRATES
LUX. — LUXEMBOURG

Falkland Is. (U.K.)

South Georgia (U.K.)

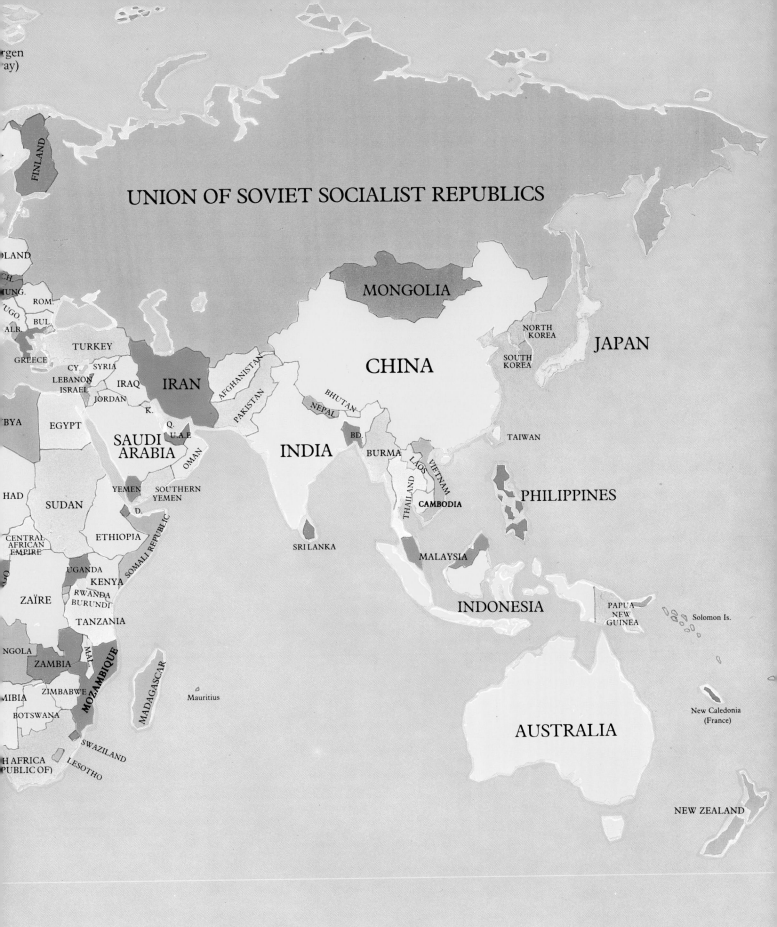

gen
ay)

FINLAND

UNION OF SOVIET SOCIALIST REPUBLICS

OLAND

CH.

HUNG.

ROM.

UGO.

BUL.

ALB.

MONGOLIA

NORTH
KOREA

JAPAN

TURKEY

GREECE

CY.

SYRIA

LEBANON

ISRAEL

IRAQ

JORDAN

IRAN

AFGHANISTAN

PAKISTAN

CHINA

SOUTH
KOREA

BYA

EGYPT

K.

Q.

U.A.E

SAUDI
ARABIA

OMAN

INDIA

BHUTAN

NEPAL

BD.

BURMA

TAIWAN

LAOS

VIETNAM

THAILAND

CAMBODIA

PHILIPPINES

HAD

SUDAN

YEMEN

SOUTHERN
YEMEN

D.

ETHIOPIA

SOMALI REPUBLIC

SRI LANKA

CENTRAL
AFRICAN
EMPIRE

UGANDA

KENYA

RWANDA
BURUNDI

MALAYSIA

ZAÏRE

TANZANIA

INDONESIA

PAPUA
NEW
GUINEA

Solomon Is.

NGOLA

ZAMBIA

MAL.

MOZAMBIQUE

MADAGASCAR

Mauritius

MIBIA

ZIMBABWE

BOTSWANA

SWAZILAND

New Caledonia
(France)

AUSTRALIA

H AFRICA
PUBLIC OF)

LESOTHO

NEW ZEALAND

ANTARCTICA

45

Index

Illustrators
Mike Atkinson, Jim Dugdale, Ron Jobson
and Roger Payne.

Cover illustrations by
Brian Watson/Linden Artists

British Library Cataloguing in Publication Data

Dempsey, Michael W. (Michael William)
    The World of geography.
    I. Title II. James, Ian
    910

    ISBN 0-7235-4322-4

Copyright © 1990 World International Publishing Limited.
All rights reserved. Published in Great Britain by
World International Publishing Limited,
an Egmont Company, Egmont House, PO Box 111,
Great Ducie Street, Manchester M60 3BL.

Printed in Singapore.

ISBN 0 7235 4322 4